I0808524

DID YOU KNOW?

Otters

DID YOU KNOW?

Otters

young reed

Contents

What is an Otter?

- Otters are **mammals** belonging to the **carnivore** family.
- They are covered in **fur** and they give birth to **live young** that feed on **mum's milk** in the first few months of life.

Polecats (left, above) and Wolverines (left, below) are related to Otters.

- Within the carnivore family, otters are included in a 'subfamily' called the **mustelids**. Their closest relations include **weasels, badgers, polecats and wolverines.**

Otters.

Facts and figures

- There are **thirteen different species** of otters around the world.
- The largest of these is the **Giant Otter** of South America, which can grow to more than **two metres** in length. The smallest is the **Asian Small-clawed Otter**, which can measure barely **sixty centimetres**.
- The Sea Otter is the heaviest species – a male can weigh up to **forty-five kilograms**.
- Many Otters are **nocturnal**, only emerging to hunt after dark, or **crespuscular**, meaning that they are active at sunrise and sunset.
- Often the only signs of their presence are their **footprints** and their distinctive, long, fishy-smelling poos, which are known as **spraints**.

Otter tracks and spraint.

Giant Otter.

Getting around

- Otters are expert swimmers, reaching speeds of **fifteen kilometres per hour** and diving to depths of **twenty metres**.

- Despite having rather short legs, Otters can **run fast** on land, sometimes at speeds of **fifty kilometres per hour** in short bursts.

- A hunting Otter can travel up to **thirty kilometres in one night** in search of food.

Special adaptations

- An Otter has **thick fur**, which traps a layer of air underneath for **warmth** and to help with **buoyancy** when swimming.

- Otters have **webbed feet** – just like a duck! – to help them swim more quickly through the water.

- The **long slender body** is also ideally adapted for swimming.

- **Sharp teeth** grab on to wet slippery prey such as fish.

Where do they live?

- Otters are familiar in zoos and animal parks across the world, and **wild Otters** have a huge range across the **Americas, Eurasia and Africa**. They are absent from few countries, such as Australia and New Zealand.

Some Otters are city dwellers, like here in Singapore.

- Otters live in and around waterways such as **rivers, lakes** and **seashores.**
- Most prefer **wild places** away from humans, although some have taken up residence in **big cities** such as Singapore and London.
- During the daytime they often stay hidden in an **underground shelter** called a **holt.**

Otters shelter in a holt, which may be a comfortable space between rocks or among tree roots, or even an old pipe.

Most Otters prefer to live around quieter rivers and lakes.

Sea Otters often gather together in 'rafts'.

Taking to the sea

- Several Otter species will happily hunt in either fresh-water habitats or along sea shores, but in the North Pacific the Sea Otter **specialises** in living in the **ocean** and can **spend its whole life at sea**.

- Sea Otters have a **heavier body** and **thicker fur** than other Otter species, to help them stay warm in the cold ocean.

- These Otters often **float on their back** in the water, resting their **food on their belly**, and sometimes gather in **rafts** containing hundreds of animals.

Sea Otter.

Eurasian Otter hunting along the seashore.

Family life

- Many Otters **live alone**, apart from when a female is looking after her young.
- A few species are **social**, with **extended family groups** of up to **ten or fifteen animals** living and hunting together.
- A litter often contains **two or three** baby Otters, which are known as a **cubs**.
- The young stay with mum for **six months**, while they learn how to hunt and survive on their own.

Some Otter species are social and hang out in extended family groups.

A youngster resting on mum.

Otter cubs learn a lot by playing with their brothers and sisters.

Sea Otter cub hitching a ride with mum.

A young Otter cub looks like a fluffy miniature version of the adult.

What's for dinner?

- Otters are **carnivores**, feeding on other animals.
- Fish make up a big part of the diet of many Otter species – they are **quick and agile swimmers** underwater in order to catch their prey.
- They also eat **insects**, **crustaceans** such as crabs, **molluscs** including water snails, **birds**, **reptiles**, **amphibians** and small **mammals**.
- Sea Otters feed mainly on **clams**, **mussels**, **sea urchins** and **crabs**, rather than fish.

Threats to Otters

- Humans are the main threat to Otters, due to the destruction and pollution of their habitat and road-traffic casualties.

Main image: oil pollution.

Plastic waste.

- Five of the thirteen Otter species are classified as **endangered** and threatened with extinction.

Beware Otters crossing.

Bear.

- **Natural predators** of Otters include **Bears, Crocodiles, Sharks** and **Orcas.**

- Thankfully Otters are still **common** in many places, and some populations are **increasing.**

First published in 2025 by New Holland Publishers

newhollandpublishers.com

Copyright © 2025 Reed New Holland Publishers
Copyright © 2025 in images: Shutterstock.com unless otherwise stated

All rights reserved. No part of this publication may be reproduced, stored in retrieval system or transmitted, in any form or by any means, electronic, mechanical, photocopying, recording or otherwise, without the prior written permission of the publishers and copyright holders.

A record of this book is held at the National Library of Australia.

ISBN 9781760798093

OTHER TITLES IN THE 'DID YOU KNOW?' SERIES:

Capybara
ISBN 9781760798048
Dolphins
ISBN 9781921078000
Kangaroos
ISBN 9781921073861
Koala
ISBN 9781921073878
Lizards
ISBN 9781921073885
Meerkat
ISBN 9781921073892
Penguins
ISBN 9781921073908
Quokka
ISBN 9781760798109
Red Panda
ISBN 9781921073915
Sharks
ISBN 9781921078017
Tasmanian Devil
ISBN 9781760798055

For details of these books and hundreds of other Natural History titles see newhollandpublishers.com